COLLEGE LIBRARY

Please return this book by the date stamped
Qif recalled, the loan is reduced to 10 d

Fines are payable for late return

4M Publications

20 Dover Street, Southwell, Notts. NG25 0EZ
Tel/Ans/Fax: 01636 813674
e-mail: four.m.publications@btinternet.com

First published by 4M Publications 2002

ISBN 0 9530494 4 2

Further copies may be obtained from 4M Publications
at the address given above.
Discounts for quantity - please enquire

®*MBTI and Myers Briggs Type Indicator are registered trademarks of
Consulting Psychologists Press, Inc. Further information and details of
Publications, Training and Qualifying Requirements are obtainable from
the Oxford Psychologist Press Ltd. (OPP), Elsfield Hall, 15-17 Elsfield
Way, Oxford OX2 8EP Tel: 01865 404500*

Malcolm Goldsmith is a Myers Briggs Consultant

Printed by Roy Allen Print Ltd., Forest Road, New Ollerton, Newark,
Notts. NG22 9PL

Contents

Part A

What is a team?
What does it have to offer?

Many of us spend a great part of our working life working in teams. It is therefore important that they work well and do what they are supposed to do, or what we require them to do. This is partly because they are expensive to maintain and operate, and partly because we invest a great deal of ourselves in them. Most of us want our working life to be enjoyable and productive, so it is important that the teams that we belong to operate as well as they can.

So what are the purposes and values of teams?

❖ They can provide an important source of stimulation for our thinking and actions at work. They can provide the 'buzz' which makes our jobs worthwhile and which enables us to work creatively and productively.

4

❖ They can usually provide us with better ideas, solutions and processes than we are likely to come up with when left to ourselves.

❖ They can help us to feel that we belong and that we can relate to other people.

❖ They can provide a structure which encourages other people to become involved.

❖ They provide a framework within which we can address issues of conflict and conflict resolution.

❖ They can provide opportunities for individuals to develop leadership and partnership working skills, and allow us to define individual areas of autonomy.

So, teams can be a good thing - but only if they work!

There can be many different sorts of team. It is important that we are able to distinguish different types and what their function or purpose is.

❖ *There is the informal group approach* - "Come on everybody, we are all in this together". This usually means we are not all in it together, in the same way or to the same depth, but do come and join those of us who want to be doing this!

❖ *There are traditional hierarchical patterns of working* where, every so often, people are brought together and informed by a senior person that "we are, after all, a team, you know". This usually happens when senior management has not got its own way and only wishes to pass on information.

❖ *There are problem-solving task forces,* specifically set up for a limited period to do a particular job. Everyone is intended and expected to pull their weight in this arrangement.

❖ *There are also committees,* charged with the task of running a particular organisation or of steering a particular piece of work through to the next stage. These are usually ongoing and may or may not function as a team (and may or may not be intended to function as a team).

❖ *There are teams which are organised to carry forward a particular piece of work;* this may be something small and specific or it may be the whole focus and object of the organisation. Perhaps the majority of 'work place teams' fall into this category and *this is the sort of team which will be the particular focus for much of this booklet,* though obviously much of what appears in these pages will be applicable to other sorts of teams.

It is important that people recognise the sort of team that they belong to, for only when we know what we are basically about can we begin to assess whether we are functioning well and effectively or not.

2   Is this your team?

- ❖ It is collectively responsible for a clear and identifiable area of work. This may be within an organisation or it may be the whole organisation itself.

- ❖ Its aims or goals are clear and it is possible to assess whether the team is succeeding in meeting them.

- ❖ It contains members with varying degrees of skills, abilities, experiences and problem solving strategies.

- ❖ There is little or no difference in status between the members.

- ❖ There are opportunities for team members to interact and meet both easily and frequently, formally and informally.

- ❖ It is structured in such a way that each member has independent job responsibilities, *and knows what these are.*

❖ Notwithstanding that, there is a fair amount of cross activity, which means that other members of the team are able to understand and, if needs be, carry out other people's job responsibilities - at least on a short-term basis.

❖ It has the authority to make decisions about how to get the work done. That is, it is empowered to pursue its goals.

❖ It experiences a mixture of individual and team "rewards". There is satisfaction for the team member both in their individual and joint work and there are ways of recognising this.

❖ The team is given frequent offers of help, assistance and encouragement from "outsiders" such as managers, trainers and other external resource people.

It is highly unlikely that such a team can function effectively with more than ten members and it is probable that it has considerably fewer. Larger numbers suggest that there may be possibilities for breaking the work down into more than one team.

3 | What makes an efficient and effective team?

✔ Well defined aims and objectives.

✔ Clear procedures to identify and resolve problems and conflicts as they occur. This is seen as being 'mainstream work' and not an occasional hiccup which they were neither expecting nor prepared for.

✔ A clear pattern for team meetings (see pages 15 and 16).

✔ A system for sharing information with each other and with external bodies.

✔ Agreed ways of monitoring its work.

Good teams provide a framework that encourages individual members, and the whole group, to work in ways which stimulate and support even more effective and efficient ways to achieve the goals that they are committed to.

4 What do teams offer to individual workers?

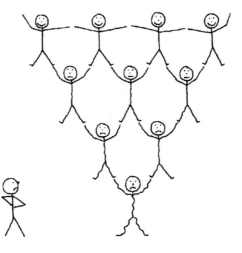

🖐 *Team members* support one another and thus build up a sense of belonging, shared responsibility and shared endeavour.

🖐 *Team members* provide each other with a certain amount of positive challenge and critical feedback which can encourage a higher level of performance.

🖐 *A team* provides a framework within which conflict can be dealt with in a constructive manner, which can help to de-personalise the conflict and focus upon the issues.

🖐 *Teams* can provide individual members with sufficient recognition and reward to make them want to belong, and continue to belong, to this working group.

-   ***Teams*** can often receive recognition from external bodies in ways that individuals (by themselves) don't.

-   ***Teams*** can often recognise and actively address threats to the work (or to individual members) from the external environment in ways that are seldom possible for individual members. They can also attract funding or exploit special opportunities.

-   ***Teams*** can develop and maintain good and constructive relationships with other teams and individuals that they relate to.

-   ***Teams*** can attract new members with desired skills who are excited by the possibility of working in an efficient and effective team.

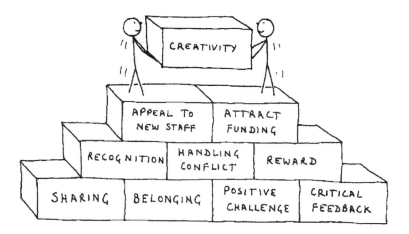

5 | Do you know what your team is for?

Keeping focused on the aims and objectives of any organisation is a constant challenge. The same can be said about teams.

A useful word to remind us of the goals of teamwork is **MAPS**.

Goals are: **M** easurable
                 A ttainable
                 P erformance related, and
                 S pecific

Measurable: Make sure that you have devised ways of measuring how effective you are as a team. There are always ways of setting criteria by which you can measure your output or effectiveness. Make sure that you have agreed these. They can be invaluable in times of difficulty and conflict resolution.

Attainable: The team as a whole, together with individual members of the team, should feel that the goals that have been set are, in fact, attainable. Goals which are not attainable sow the seeds of disaffection and disenchantment amongst staff. Goals which are not only achievable but also achieved promote a sense of well-being and worth amongst members and give opportunities for recognition from external bodies, outside the immediate team.

Performance related: Each member of the team should be able to see that their own work contributes to and is related to achieving the goals of the team. An inability to see how your work makes a difference can lead to a sense of job dissatisfaction, with all the ancillary problems which so often spring from that such as absenteeism, poor work record, declining morale and a lack of identity with the team and possibly with colleagues.

Specific: Goals should be spelled out and be as specific as possible. General 'goodwill' or 'progress' or 'increased sales/attendance' are not enough. There should be identifiable targets, or goals that are accepted and then 'owned' by the members of the team. Being specific often involves more work in the early stages, but the impact that it can have on team morale and commitment are well worth the extra effort.

Another acronym which is often used is **SMART**, which stands for

Note the emphasis upon the team's objectives being grounded, not lost in some well-meaning and good-sounding generalities.

It is a good idea to try and sub-divide your team's objectives, making them as specific and as realistic as possible. In that way it is more likely that you can see that they are measurable. *Whenever you think that it is impossible to measure your team's performance, ask yourself if you have broken its tasks down sufficiently.*

6 Questions that teams need to ask themselves

? Who are our customers / clients / patients? Who will benefit if all our work goes well?

? Who is it that 'supplies' the raw material / data / people that we are working with? If the first question (above) relates to what happens *after* our work, then this question seeks to identify what happens *before* our team's contribution.

? Who are the competitors in the field? Is there anything that can be learned from them?

? What additional people or groups do we have to deal with, and how do we assess their relationship with us?

? Is it possible to say how people outside the team view us, in terms of our effectiveness, efficiency and general morale?

? Reflecting on the different relationships that the team has with individuals or other groups:
        - which should it try to benefit from more
        - which does it need to improve ?

? In the light of the above question,
who will now do *what, to* or *with whom* and *by when,*
in order to help the team with what it has decided needs to be done?

7 Team meetings - how efficient and effective are they?

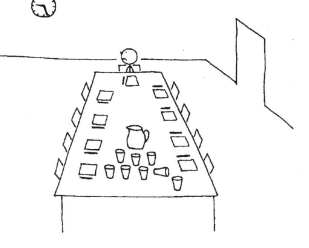

Team meetings can be a source of intense frustration or irritation. They can also be a much valued and eagerly anticipated opportunity to share views and to give and receive mutual support and encouragement. They are also an indispensable vehicle for communication.

If they are not one already, then team meetings need to become a most valued resource.

Check out your experience against the list that follows. It is not implied that all teams meet in the same way, but you may find a checklist like this helps you think about the strengths and weaknesses of your own team.

- Is the purpose of the meeting clear to everyone in advance?
- Is an agenda provided in advance? Does it it encourage or discourage discussion?
- Is the agenda followed during the meeting, or basically ignored?
- Is it clear who is and who is not expected to attend?
- Do members attend regularly?
- Do they turn up on time?
- Is the meeting room appropriate for the business in hand?
- Are the meetings given a priority or are they regularly interrupted?
- Do team members come to the meetings prepared?
- Does everyone feel free to participate? Does everyone?
- Do all the members of the team understand their roles and their responsibilities?
- Is there enough time? Is it too short (what frustrations follow?) or too long (what frustrations follow?) ?
- Do members really listen to one another?
- Are the meetings chaired efficiently and effectively?
- Are there any opportunities to reflect on the *process* of the meeting?
- Do there appear to be too many times when 'hidden agendas' are being played out?
- Does the team over-depend upon the leader, or facilitator (if there is one)?
- Is the amount of material covered at each meeting appropriate? What happens if it is not, and how does the team prevent it happening again?
- Are minutes written up and distributed to team members soon after the meeting?
- Do the minutes accurately summarise the meeting?
- Are decisions that are made followed up after the meeting, quickly and effectively?
- Are ground rules for the meetings known and adhered to?
- Is the effectiveness of the meetings monitored in any way?

8   What about your team - is it efficient and effective?

How effective is your team?
Are you pleased to be a member of it?

Does it provide you with stimulation, support and encouragement, positive critical feedback, rewards and a sense of belonging and wellbeing?

Every team has its periods of up and down; problems are inevitable; some conflicts are unavoidable. What matters is knowing that you have strategies to deal with them when they occur so that they can be (eventually) team-building experiences rather than team-destroying disasters.

Complete this questionnaire about your team.

*Put a circle around 5 if you **strongly agree** with the statement*
*Put a circle round 1 if you **strongly disagree***
Circle 2, 3 or 4 accordingly if your response is between these two

*(The **higher** your score the **more positive** you are about the statement)*

MY TEAM .....

1 ..... has well defined aims and objectives:
   I know what we are about   1   2   3   4   5

2 ..... has clear (formal or informal) procedures
   for identifying and resolving problems
   and conflicts as they occur   1   2   3   4   5

3 ..... has no real difficulties in sharing
   information with its members and
   with external bodies   1   2   3   4   5

4 ..... has ways of monitoring its effectiveness
   and efficiency   1   2   3   4   5

5 ..... contains members with varying degrees
   of skills, abilities and experiences   1   2   3   4   5

6 ..... is not handicapped by problems relating
   to the status of different members   1   2   3   4   5

7 ..... has plenty of opportunities to meet and
   interact, both formally and informally   1   2   3   4   5

Total c/f: _____

8 ..... is structured in such a way that each
member has clear and independent job
responsibilities, and knows what these
are   **1   2   3   4   5**

9 ..... is structured in such a way that, certainly
for a short period, members can stand in
for one another, understanding and being
able to perform their job responsibilities   **1   2   3   4   5**

10 ..... has the authority to make appropriate
decisions about how to get its work done   **1   2   3   4   5**

11 ..... provides me with interest and stimulation,
making my job seem worthwhile and
encouraging me to work creatively and
productively   **1   2   3   4   5**

12 ..... comes up with ideas, solutions and
processes - almost certainly more than
if we were working alone   **1   2   3   4   5**

13 ..... encourages other people to become
involved   **1   2   3   4   5**

14 ..... provides opportunities for me to take
control of my own work   **1   2   3   4   5**

15 ..... provides opportunities for exercising
leadership skills in appropriate areas   **1   2   3   4   5**

16 ..... encourages a sense of belonging, shared
responsibility and shared endeavour   **1   2   3   4   5**

17 ..... provides me with a secure framework
within which I can both receive and give
critical feedback   **1   2   3   4   5**

18 ..... makes me feel/think that I am doing
a worthwhile job in a worthwhile joint
enterprise   **1   2   3   4   5**

19 ..... provides me with sufficient
affirmation/rewards/strokes   **1   2   3   4   5**

20 ..... is the sort of team that other people would
like to join   **1   2   3   4   5**

21 ..... has ways of knowing when it is doing
things well (or not so well)   **1   2   3   4   5**

22 ..... does not place unreasonable and
unattainable expectations on my work   **1   2   3   4   5**

23 ..... enables me to see how my work fits into
the wider picture, and recognises its
importance   **1   2   3   4   5**

24 ..... provides me with a sense of worth; I enjoy
being a part of it and contributing to it   **1   2   3   4   5**

Total c/f _____

25 ..... meets regularly for worthwhile team
     meetings   **1 2 3 4 5**

26 ..... encourages us to listen to one another;
     everyone is valued   **1 2 3 4 5**

27 ..... does not operate on a system of
     favouritism or hidden agendas   **1 2 3 4 5**

28 ..... benefits from creative, effective and
     accessible leadership   **1 2 3 4 5**

29 ..... is fun!   **1 2 3 4 5**

30 ..... is great to belong to   **1 2 3 4 5**

Now add up your scores for all 30 questions   **Full total** _____

If you scored 150 - Have you ever thought about writing a book on teamwork, you have much experience and insight to share!

If you scored 120 or more - Your team is going well; can you identify the areas which need to be improved

If you scored between 90 and 119 - You have a reasonably effective team but it clearly falls down in some major areas. These need to be identified and addressed.

If you scored between 60 and 89 - You have major problems. It is imperative that they are addressed. Probably your team needs an outside facilitator. You are going to have to invest some time and money into the enterprise otherwise the work will not get done effectively and efficiently and the team members will not be wholly satisfied and will have at least one eye on the situations vacant columns - this may come as a relief to you, but what if you are the problem and what if their replacement turns out to be even worse!

If you scored less than 60 - What team?   Return to the start and do not collect £200.   You have real problems and need to begin at square one and think through the whole process of team building from the beginning again.

One way of developing teams is by building on the insights and experience of understanding personality.   The remainder of this booklet is devoted to showing how an understanding of the Myers Briggs Type Indicator can be a stimulating and liberating way of understanding and experiencing teamwork.

Part B

9 **Understanding Personality - the Myers Briggs Type Indicator**

Teams are made up of people.

Sometimes they get on with each other really well, stimulate and encourage one another. Sometimes they seem to rub each other up the wrong way and all manner of conflicts arise.

Perhaps if we could find a way of understanding what makes people 'tick' then it might be possible to find ways of ensuring that we can deal with problem scenarios and turn unpromising situations into times of creativity.

The ®Myers Briggs Type Indicator (MBTI) provides us with just such a tool.

It is something which points out or *indicates* different *Types* of personality. It is called the *Myers Briggs* Type Indicator because it was devised by Isabel Myers and her mother Katharine Briggs. They worked in America early last century and their work paralleled work done at a similar time by Carl Jung who published his book on Personality Types in 1923.

Since it came onto the market in 1975 the MBTI has become the world's most-used tool for understanding personality and it is estimated that world-wide, well over two million people a year complete the questionnaire.

This booklet does not claim to replace the process of exploring your own personality via the MBTI. But it does offer you some of the insights that can be gained from an understanding of personality, especially in relation to working together in teams.

The Myers Briggs Type Indicator is a non-threatening and thoroughly enjoyable way of gaining understanding about how different types of personalities interact with each other. It offers valuable insight into the gifts that different types of people bring to their work situation and suggests how and when they need the gifts that other people have to offer.

---o---o---o---o---o---

'What's it all about?'

We are either left or right handed. For most people this is not something that they give much thought to, it just happens to be how they are. When we pick up a pen to sign our name we do not stop and ask ourselves which hand we will use to write with, we make that choice subconsciously.

Similarly we either enjoy or do not enjoy watching football, prefer classical music to pop music, prefer ice-cream to ice-lollies - or prefer not to have either.

That is, the whole of life is made up of choices, most of which we seldom think about; we are, as it were on 'automatic'. Much the same can be said about the way that our personalities develop.

We subconsciously make a whole range of choices day by day and, added together, these choices make us the sort of person that we are. This is the person who goes to work and who relates to a whole host of other people who are also making subconscious preferences. Perhaps they like to plan ahead or leave things until the last minute. Perhaps they are bored by too much detail or they may relish small print and spotting factual errors. Perhaps they like their desk cleared when they have finished a piece of work or they may work on lots of different things apparently at the same time. They may tell you frequently how much they appreciate you or perhaps you have never heard them express a single word of gratitude. You may know all about their families and their likes and dislikes or perhaps you have worked with them for years and hardly know them any better now than when you first met them.

All this demonstrates something that you already know - that people are different!

The Myers Briggs Type Indicator provides us with a tool which can help explain some of these differences and demonstrate why we get on better with some people than we do with others; why some people irritate us and others interest us.

It also explains why we ourselves might be highly irritating to some people. It is not that we have something wrong with us, that somehow we are flawed or inadequate, it is just that we are different and because of this we relate more easily to some people than we do to others - and they to us.

The only bits of jargon that you need to understand

This section contains the heart of the theory of the MBTI. It is not difficult to understand, but -

> *to make the best use of the rest of this booklet you really do need to familiarise yourself with just eight words and symbols and what they represent.*

They are used here in a technical sense and so may have slightly different meanings to how you have understood them in the past.

They can be set out in four sets of pairs:

Extravert (E)	and	*Introvert (I)*
Senser (S)	and	*Intuitive (N)*
Thinker (T)	and	*Feeler (F)*
Judger (J)	and	*Perceiver (P)*

Putting the jargon to good effect

Extraverts are people who are energised or stimulated by the outside world around them. They enjoy engaging with people or situations or events, they feel 'pulled' by what is going on outside and beyond them. They are often quite talkative, they share a great deal in terms of ideas and information (about themselves as well as about other people and things). They tend to express their emotions reasonably freely. It is said of them that they add breadth to life.

Within the work situation - *Extraverts:*

- Like variety and action
- Tend to work faster and be impatient with complications

- Are often good at greeting people
- Tend to dislike long and slow jobs
- Don't mind the telephone
- Like to have people around them
- Can be drained or bored if left on their own for too long
- Speak out easily (and often) at meetings
- Are relatively easy to get to know
- Regard action as more important than thought

There is something of the extravert in all of us, but some people prefer this to be their basic, 'default' position, whilst others reflect that they really prefer their introvert (see next paragraphs) character to be their basic, 'default' position.

We use the letter E to represent Extravert or extraversion.

Introverts are people who are energised or stimulated by their inner world of thoughts and ideas. They can experience the outer world as being rather oppressive and the need to relate to different people and situations can be quite tiring for them. They do not easily express their emotions in ways that others can quickly appreciate and they can be quite diffident at sharing personal information - or even information about ideas, people or events that might be seen as being part of the job that they are doing.

They can be quite reflective and think things over before they speak.

The extravert tends to think as he or she is speaking - they are thinking out their position as they speak. The introvert tends to sort things out in their mind before speaking, so when they do speak we are hearing a measured and thoughtful response.

Within the work situation, *Introverts*

- Like quiet for concentration
- Tend to be careful about detail and do not make sweeping statements
- Don't mind working on the same thing for a long time
- Often dislike the telephone and its interruptions
- Can find that spending too much time with people, especially strangers, can be quite draining
- Are content to work alone
- Tend to hold back at meetings and may have difficulties 'getting into' a discussion
- Tend to take longer to get to know
- Can be so deep in thought that they fail to act

Extraverts are often referred to by using the letter **E** and Introverts are often referred to by using the letter **I**.

All of us are both extravert and introvert - but we prefer one to the other. It is worth trying to work out what you think you are, and then what you think the people that you work with are.

I think that I am probably an _____

Now write down the names of 5 colleagues and try and assess what you think they are

1   _____   E or I

2   _____   E or I

3   _____   E or I

4   _____   E or I

5   _____   E or I

The next pair of words is *Intuitive* and *Senser.*

These relate to the ways in which we take in information from the world around us. Some people use their senses (hearing, seeing, feeling, smelling and touching) whilst other people seem to have a general hunch, they 'intuit' the information that they need.

Sensers are aware of specific things that come to them via their senses and they are aware of the facts of their present experience. They tend to look at specific parts, they live in the immediate present and they prefer handling practicalities. If we translate this into the work situation, *Sensers*:

- Like established routines
- Dislike new problems unless there are standard ways of solving them
- Tend to be good at precise work
- Usually work their way through an issue to the conclusion
- Read instructions!
- See 'what is'
- Seldom make errors of fact
- Are quick to grasp details
- See the objections to new ideas before they see the good points
- Tend to be specific and literal when speaking or writing

Intuitives become aware of things via their 'sixth sense' or hunches or intuition. They are interested in the pattern or the meaning of things and tend to see the 'big picture' rather than the details. Intuitives live for the future, imagining possibilities. If we translate this into the work situation, *Intuitives*:

- Dislike routine
- Like solving new problems
- Dislike detailed work because it takes up too much time
- Jump to conclusions
- Read instructions as a last resort (if they can find them or understand them)
- See 'what might be'
- Often make errors of fact
- Tend to disregard details
- Are easily seduced by new ideas without recognising inherent problems
- Are general or abstract when speaking or writing

Everyone is both a Senser and an Intuitive depending upon circumstances, but we all prefer operating in one mode rather than the other. See if you can work out which you are and then what the people you work with might be.

Sensing is often referred to by the letter **S** and Intuition is often referred to by the letter **N**. (I know that Intuition begins with an 'I' but we have already used I for Introvert!).

I think that I am probably a (an) _____

Now write down the names of 5 colleagues and try and assess what you think they are

1 _____   S or N

2 _____   S or N

3 _____   S or N

4 _____   S or N

5 _____   S or N

The third pair of words is *Thinking* and *Feeling*.

These relate to the ways in which we process the information that we have taken in (either through our senses or through our intuition). We process the information either through a cerebral or thinking route or through an emotional or feeling route.

N.B. It is important that we do not make a hasty leap here and falsely assume that if we say that someone operates through a feeling process then we are implying that they are unintelligent; and if we say that someone operates via a thinking process then we are implying that they have no emotions!

People who are *Thinkers* make decisions on the basis of objective considerations and logic. The thinker will tend to be concerned about truth and justice. He or she will tend to see things from the outside, looking in, and will take a long, cool look at things.

People who are *Feelers* make decisions on the basis of subjective personal values. They are concerned with person-centred values and they seek harmony and place great store on human values and emotions. They tend to see thing from the inside, as a participant rather than as a (thinking) observer.

Thinkers can seem cold and perhaps condescending to Feelers, and Feelers may seem to be emotional and muddled to Thinkers!

From the perspective of the work situation, *Thinkers:*

- Are relatively unemotional and uninterested in people's feelings
- May hurt people without realising it
- May seem to be hard-hearted

- Can get along without harmony
- Need to be treated fairly
- Dislike or ignore the irrational parts of behaviour
- Tend to make their decisions impersonally, perhaps ignoring people's wishes and feelings
- When situations require it, are able to reprimand or sack people
- Good at assessing logical, impersonal consequences of decisions and actions

Whilst, from the perspective of work, *Feelers:*

- Tend to be very aware of other people and their feelings
- Enjoy pleasing people
- Tend to be sympathetic
- Want harmony
- Need praise (at least occasionally)
- Understand and take the irrational into account
- Often let their decisions be influenced by their own or other people's wishes
- Can be easily hurt
- Have difficulty telling people unpleasant things
- Good at assessing human consequences of decisions or actions

Everyone is both a Thinker and a Feeler but we prefer, are more at ease, with one approach rather than the other.

Thinkers are often referred to by the letter **T** and Feelers by the letter **F.**

I think that I am probably a _____

Now write down the names of 5 colleagues and try and assess what you think they are

1   _____   T or F

2   _____   T or F

3   _____   T or F

4   _____   T or F

5   _____   T or F

The final pair of words and letters that we need to think about are *Judger* and *Perceiver.* These words relate to the end product of all our deliberations, the ways in which we show or display the sort of personalities that we have.

People who are *Judgers* like to draw boundaries, like things to be settled, like to know just where things are. Judgers tend to be reliable, dependable; they are the backbone of any organisation. They maintain the traditions, play by the book, and can be quite decisive.

In contrast to this . . . .

People who are *Perceivers* like to keep their options open, are uncomfortable with closure and operate on the provisional. The Perceiver does not like to say 'No', has trouble with boundaries, likes to try everything and endeavours to keep many balls in the air at the same time.

In the work situation *Judgers:*

- Dislike interrupting one task for another, preferring to work to a schedule

- Want authority, structure and predictability
- Aim to be right, and to master something
- Tend to be rated as effective managers
- Live according to plans, customs and objectives
- Are best when they can plan their work and stick to that plan
- May be slow to see the need for change and reluctant to adapt plans
- Can be satisfied once they have reached a decision
- May come to decisions too quickly and ignore evidence to the contrary
- Tend to be comfortable in hierarchical organisations, which have authority, structure and predictability

Whilst, in the work situation *Perceivers:*

- Start many projects, and may have difficulty in finishing them, postponing unpleasant tasks
- Want autonomy, variety and stimulation
- Aim to miss nothing and try everything
- Don't mind leaving things open for last minute alterations
- Tend to be rated as creative professionals
- Live according to the moment and adjust relatively easily to the unexpected
- Tend to be good at adapting to changing situations
- May get bored easily and seek change for change's sake
- Remain curious and welcome new information even when a decision has been reached
- Have difficulty in making decisions - and sticking to them
- Tend to be resistant to authority, which can lead to under-performance in hierarchical organisations

Everybody is part Judger and part Perceiver - but we prefer one to the other.

Judgers are often referred to by the letter **J** and Perceivers by the letter **P**.

I think that I am probably a _____

Now write down the names of 5 colleagues and try and assess what you think they are

1   _____   J or P

2   _____   J or P

3   _____   J or P

4   _____   J or P

5   _____   J or P

Now bring together your four letters and you will be describing your personality type.

You will be, for example an ESTJ, or an INFP, or an ENTP - which, in longhand would be:

> An extraverted sensing thinking judger (ESTJ), or
>
> an introverted intuitive feeling perceiver (INFP) or
>
> an extraverted intuitive thinking perceiver (ENTP).

There are sixteen possible combination of letters. We shall come back to these later, on page 63.

Try and work out the personality type of your closest colleagues - if several of you are using this booklet it might be a good idea to stop here and discuss with each other how you have described one another, and see if you can come to a common mind.

I think that my Type is probably _____

Now write down the names of 5 colleagues and try and assess what you think their Types probably are

1   _____   _____

2   _____   _____

3   _____   _____

4   _____   _____

5   _____   _____

REMEMBER!

In order to discover your actual Personality Profile, according to the Myers Briggs Type Indicator, you need to complete the formal and detailed questionnaire and have its results explained to you by a professionally trained and qualified Myers Briggs practitioner.

All this booklet can do is to give you a general understanding and impression of the varieties of human personality and begin to show you how these interact upon each other within a work situation and the ways in which teams can harness these different personalities to best advantage.

If you want to learn more about the MBTI read *Knowing Me - Knowing You* by Malcolm Goldsmith and Martin Wharton, published by SPCK in 1993.

10 Needing each other

We need to make it clear that all these eight different categories are of equal worth. It is not 'better' to be an extravert than an introvert, it is not 'better' to be an intuitive than a senser.

They are different, and they are equally valid. But more than that, they are complementary.

Extraverts *need* introverts, and introverts *need* extraverts, because they each bring something special into the relationship; they each have a contribution to make. Similarly, intuitives need sensers and sensers need intuitives, thinkers need feelers and feelers need thinkers. Perceivers need judgers just as much as judgers need perceivers.

A team which was composed entirely of extraverts would miss the special contribution that the introvert can offer - it would, for example, almost certainly be weak on reflection. A team composed entirely of judgers would miss the special insights of the perceiver and would almost certainly run the risk of making too hasty judgements, deciding things before all the possibilities were explored. Similarly a team composed entirely of perceivers might struggle ever to make a decision (and once made, would almost certainly want to change it within a very short space of time!

By gaining an understanding of your own personality type it should be possible to be more aware of the specific gifts and insights that you can offer to a team, whilst at the same time recognising the gifts and insights that you need from other members.

Think through the way that you have described yourself, and your colleagues, and see how an understanding of personality type can help identify the ways in which we complement each other and bring specific gifts (and needs) to the workplace.

If you are an Extravert, you will need the help and insights that Introverts can offer:-

⇨ to help keep you focused, so that you are not so easily deflected by external stimuli

⇨ to help you explore inner depths

⇨ to help you gain more depth and concentration when sharing tasks

⇨ to help you value and make the best use of times of solitude and working alone

⇨ to make you more aware of what might be going on within yourself as you tackle various issues

⇨ to help you listen to what other people are saying - or to make you more aware of the fact that not everyone is joining in a discussion

⇨ to help you with long slow jobs

. . . . . if you are an Introvert, you will need the help and insight that Extraverts can offer:-

⇨ to help you make your views and opinions heard in meetings and discussions

⇨ to help you get to know other people - and also to help get you known by them!

⇨ to keep conversations flowing when you seem to have said everything that there is to be said

⇨ to ensure that strangers are welcomed

⇨ to break the ice at social occasions

⇨ to help you ensure that all the things that you want to communicate actually are communicated

If you are an Intuitive, you will need the help and insights that a Senser can offer:-

⇨ to bring up detailed information
⇨ to help you apply experience to current problems
⇨ to read the instructions, or the fine print in a contract
⇨ to encourage you to notice the things that need attention paying to them now!
⇨ to help you have more patience and take one step at a time
⇨ to help you keep track of essential details
⇨ to help you face current difficulties, or future possibilities, with realism
⇨ to help you keep records and know where things are
⇨ to remind you that the joys of the present are as important as the potential joys of the future

. . . . . but if you are a Senser, you will need the help and insights that an Intuitive can offer:-

⇨ to look for and expect new possibilities
⇨ to develop a vision of the future and of what it might be
⇨ to supply new and perhaps ingenious ways of looking at current problems
⇨ to help you live with alternatives
⇨ to 'read the signs' of coming change
⇨ to help you with ideas about preparing for the future
⇨ to help you share in their enthusiasms
⇨ to be open to the possibilities of vision and excitement
⇨ to show that the joys of the future are worth waiting for and planning for

If you are a Feeler you will need the help and insight that a Thinker can offer:-

⇨ to help you analyse situations and facts
⇨ to help you deal with organisational matters
⇨ to do the difficult and hard tasks so far as people are concerned
⇨ to find faults, mistakes and be critical
⇨ to 'hold the line' when opposition grows
⇨ to redefine, restructure or reform
⇨ to help you think things through objectively and not be swayed by sentiment or 'hard luck' stories
⇨ to ensure that you act fairly and without favouritism

. . . . . whilst if you are a Thinker you will need the help and insight that a Feeler can offer

⇨ to help you be aware of 'human factors' in the workplace
⇨ to conciliate and persuade people; to promote harmony
⇨ to help you understand how people feel about things
⇨ to help build up empathy
⇨ to help you appreciate people's values as well as their thoughts
⇨ to help you give a few words of thanks and praise and encouragement occasionally

Finally:

If you are a Perceiver, you will need the help and insight that a Judger can offer:-

⇨ to help you reach or make a decision
⇨ to provide some structure and routine to your work
⇨ to encourage you to have a sense of loyalty to your roots and a respect for your tradition
⇨ to help you prepare for deadlines
⇨ to assist you to recognise the benefits that can come from having an ordered lifestyle/diary/desk/filing system
⇨ to remind you that there are some ultimate authorities
⇨ to ensure that necessary jobs get done

..... whilst if you are a Judger you will need the help and insight that a Perceiver can offer:-

⇨ to help you not be too hasty in reaching a conclusion or in making a decision
⇨ to look for and appreciate all the options that may exist
⇨ to help you realise that a set-back need not necessarily be a disaster
⇨ to save you from the tyranny of routine
⇨ to help you keep authority figures and structures, hierarchies and systems in perspective
⇨ to appreciate just how much time there really is
⇨ to see rules as there to help us rather than restrict us
⇨ to have fun and to respond to the needs of the moment

What this section is concerned to show is that because people are different, they bring to the work situations and to teams the strengths and weaknesses of their personality types. No person has all the gifts, and no person has nothing which they can offer. The stronger a person's gifts in one direction, the more likely it is that he or she will need the gifts that someone else can offer who is different from them. Discovering something about our own gifts inevitably helps us to look for and appreciate the gifts that other people can bring.

Any team needs to have a balance. It needs both extraversion and introversion. It needs sensing as well as intuition. It needs both thinking and feeling, and it needs judgement and perception - and no one person is likely to provide all these, because we all prefer one option to the other - and this is what makes us different. Those differences can be infuriating to work with; the same difference can enhance and stimulate our team. It is all a matter of how we understand and harness such differences.

11 How personality differences can be used to advantage in team situations

We want to give three examples of how an understanding of personality type can assist us in the daily work of teams. There are many other examples but we shall look briefly at:

Communication
Setting goals
Resolving conflict

Understanding personalities will not do the work for you in these areas of concern, but can give you some tools, some insights or ways into exploring the subject and perhaps help you to reach a more imaginative approach.

1. Communication

People do not 'hear' in the same way. They are looking for or wanting different things. If we are trying to persuade them, convince them or explain something to them then it is important that we use words, images and an approach which actually does 'communicate'.

We need to remember that, when we are trying to persuade someone it is *them* that we are trying to persuade, not ourselves. So we need to fashion our words and our approach in ways that meet them where *they* are.

So, *when communicating with people who are Sensers,* remember the sort of things that Sensers like and the things which they find difficult.

- be factual
- show that this approach has worked in the past
  (it is not just speculation)
- as far as possible reduce all the risk factors
- be able to show why it makes sense
- work out all the details in advance

Remember - Sensers are rooted in reality, they don't warm to grandiose ideas, they like facts, sequences, reality and dependability.

When communicating with people who are Intuitives, remember the things that Intuitives like and how they differ from Sensers .....

- outline a global vision
- stress the importance of not missing this opportunity
- be enthusiastic and argue with confidence
- indicate the challenge
- point out future benefits

Remember - Intuitives are excited by future possibilities; don't give them too many facts or you may bore them or confuse them - they don't want the detail they want the overall picture. Intuitives like to be 'different' and they are fascinated by the 'new'.

When communicating with people who are Thinkers remember the things that Thinkers like and how they differ from Feelers

- be logical
- go easy on the passion and enthusiasm (though recognise that they may also be Intuitives)
- spell out the principles involved
- exude competence
- spell out the costs and benefits

Remember - Thinkers are wary of emotion, so no matter how committed you are and excited by what you wish to communicate, their concern is with the facts and the logical development of your argument. Thinkers like to be valued for their cool and logical appraisal of situations and plans.

When communicating with people who are Feelers

- be personable and friendly - ask about the cat or their cold or their holiday!
- tell them who else is in favour of the idea
- indicate how helpful and user-friendly your idea is
- explain that it's the 'right' thing to do
- stress the value of what you are suggesting and the benefits that it might bring to others

Remember - Feelers like to be in relationship with people, so if you want them really to 'hear' you, then you need to establish 'contact' with

45

them. Take an interest in them as people, 'share' with them. They are more likely to respond to you if they feel that they like you and that you like them.

It is helpful to bear these 'typological insights' in mind when you are discussing things with different members of your team.

Remember, <u>saying</u> the same thing to different people is different from <u>communicating</u> the same thing to different people.

It is particularly important to remember these insights when you are presenting an argument or a plan to a group of people - perhaps you might be speaking in support of a funding application to a grant-making committee, or trying to persuade a management committee to follow a certain path. You might even be facing an interview committee for a new job! In these situations remember that there is likely to be a mix of different personality types on the group of people you are trying to influence. You may therefore need to present your case in slightly different ways in the same conversation. This is not an easy thing to do, but if you can manage it then you will stand a far greater chance of achieving your objectives.

Incidentally, thinking in terms of psychological type (which is what we are doing here) raises considerable questions about the current practice of ensuring (in order to be fair) that candidates for interview are asked exactly the same questions. In fact, this is patently unfair, because an extrovert will spontaneously talk freely and give you all sorts of information (much of which you haven't asked for) whilst with an introvert you may have to dig around in order to unearth the same information. *Interview procedures have a built-in bias towards favouring extraverts, so take care all you politically correct interviewers!*

2. Setting Goals

You need to know where you are wanting to go, otherwise you are unlikely to know if you have got there! Similarly, you need to know what it is that you are wanting to achieve, or else how will you know if you have achieved anything? Teams can very easily be deflected from their principal tasks unless they are clearly stated and 'owned' by everyone in the team.

An understanding of Personality Type can provide some helpful checks to help ensure that we are asking relevant questions.

☞ *Has everyone had an opportunity to speak about the goals?*
It is very easy for extraverts to dominate conversations and team meetings. Care has to be taken to ensure that introverts have the opportunity to make a contribution. They may need to be positively encouraged - saying afterwards that they had a chance to speak up if they wanted to is not enough! It may not be the team's responsibility to set the goal, but it will certainly be the team's responsibility to help achieve it, and this is where everyone's viewpoint and contribution is needed. It is a clear task of leadership to ensure that everyone is heard.

☞ *Has there been ample time to reflect upon the goals?*
This is another example of the extravert-introvert divide. Remember that extraverts 'think with their mouths', they formulate their understanding as they speak, they need to talk in order to get their minds around the issue. Introverts work in a different way. They need to have time and space to reflect. They tend to sort things out in their mind before they speak, so that when they do eventually speak it is more likely to be their considered opinion. It is therefore essential that as well as allowing time for discussion, there must also be time for reflection.

☞ *Are the goals realistic?*

This question seeks to clarify some of the tensions that can exist between Sensers and Intuitives. Intuitives are always in danger of going over the top, of escalating expectations. They can become intoxicated by ideas and may need to be reined in occasionally. Sensers tend to be rooted in reality and can provide a firm anchor when looking ahead. They are more likely to be aware of financial and other resource restraints. But - they can also apply a brake to every new idea. An important component of good team leadership is to be able to conduct a fruitful dialogue between the Intuitive and Sensing members of the team. Both are necessary.

☞ *Do the goals allow for future expansion?*

This is a necessary development of the last point. Are we able to see our immediate goals within a wider perspective, wider in the sense of seeing how they relate to other issues and also in terms of what the future possibilities might be. This is very much the gift that Intuitives have to offer. An Intuitive who is also a Extravert may willingly and eagerly share these insights with colleagues, but one who is an Introvert may need to be encouraged to share. This question also brings in some of the qualities that a Perceiver has to share because they are flexible and pliant and will have few difficulties in turning their mind to a new situation. Judgers may find this a more difficult question to cope with because, in their view, it might be outside the terms of reference that they were given.

☞ *Are the goals consistent with the organisation's mission?*

A question that the Judgers will certainly want to be explored. Judgers are, in a sense, the 'keepers of the tradition' and they are anxious to maintain the organisation and keep it true to its word and consistent with its past and thus able to meet people's expectations of it. This is a necessary question to ask. All too frequently teams can find themselves straying from the purpose for which they were set up - there may be good reasons for that, but we need to be aware of what is happening, and why. Perceivers tend to roam!

☞ *Will everyone be committed to the goals ?*
This question brings out some of the strengths and concerns of the Feelers. They are concerned to promote harmony; they want everyone to feel good and to be part of a shared endeavour. If there is doubt that everyone is committed to the cause, then the Feelers are not at ease. It is important to them that differences are talked through. It is also important to Judgers that everyone is 'loyal to the cause'. Therefore another important function of team leadership is to ensure that everyone involved shares a common commitment. Waverers need to be encouraged to share their doubts and divisions, or potential divisions, and have them dealt with as soon as possible.

☞ *Is there a plan to monitor progress?*
This is where the Thinkers can make a specific contribution. They will naturally and automatically be thinking about the process and evaluating its effectiveness. Because they can look objectively at the work in progress and do not necessarily see its success or failure as a reflection upon them, as individuals, they are more likely to be willing to encourage and 'own' a process of evaluation. Teams need an inbuilt and objective process of monitoring their life and work and Thinkers should be encouraged to provide this (with the understanding that they need to learn how to communicate their findings to those who are Feelers and who may therefore feel that any criticism of the team's performance is a criticism of them as people).

Sometimes it is more appropriate for the team leader to bring in outsiders to do the monitoring and evaluating, but even on those occasions the Thinkers in the team can be preparing the ground and helping other team members to appreciate the value of monitoring and evaluation processes.

☞ *Do the goals allow for the emergence of the new and unexpected?* Coping with the new and the unexpected is one of the strengths of Perceivers in any team. They tend to be more adaptable, more spontaneous than Judgers and if they are also Intuitives then the emergence of the new and unexpected can be a positive and healthy development for any team. Without the gifts and insights of Perceivers there is always the danger that people become defensive and resistant to change, feeling or thinking that the new is threatening.

3. Resolving Conflict

Conflict is an inevitable part of life and every team will have to face situations of conflict and learn ways of resolving it. Not all conflict is destructive, there can be positive as well as negative aspects.

☺ Looking at it positively:

▸ conflict can be a pre-requisite to change
▸ it can generate energy and activity
▸ external conflict can have an internal unifying effect
▸ expression of conflict can reduce tension and brings things out into the open

☹ On the negative side:

▸ conflict can result in polarisation, people within the team can 'take sides'
▸ it can disrupt other productive activities and use up a great deal of emotional and intellectual energy

No single personality type handles conflict better than other types, in fact conflict usually brings out the worst in all types - exaggerating what, at other times, can be strengths.

Steps through Conflict:

1. Try to define the issues. Work out exactly what it is that is causing the problem. Usually when a conflict situation arises, all sorts of other things are added onto the actual cause. There have probably been floating, unresolved issues waiting to attach themselves to a convenient crisis.

2. Try to put them into a typological framework. That is, try to separate the issues from the people involved and endeavour to see them as resulting from the personality characteristics that we have been thinking about. We shall be exploring how to do this later in this section.

3. Ask the team members involved to identify with each other's point of view. Again, move away from actual personalities and focus upon the characteristics of personality type.

4. Seek to create compromises that can move the conflict on towards resolution. We have to move from lose-lose or lose-win situations to win-win situations in which each person involved in the conflict feels that they can emerge stronger (and wiser). An understanding of personality can help in this process.

Clashes between Thinking and Feeling

Thinkers will invariably push for greater clarity, whilst Feelers are wanting harmony and feel threatened by the probing and questioning of Thinkers. In order to achieve the harmony that they desire Feelers may well hold out an olive branch which, rather than creating clarity, further muddies the water as far as the Thinker is concerned.

Thinkers may well see conflict as an inevitable process leading to creativity, so it is, for them, a valuable and necessary part of getting on with the job and clarifying issues. Feelers, however, often experience conflict as extremely stressful, emotional and upsetting. Remember - Thinkers can place themselves *outside* a situation whilst Feelers experience situations from the *inside*. Thinkers may well be able to leave the conflict in the workplace, returning to it tomorrow. Feelers will almost always take it home with them. The effective team leader will be aware of these differences and be able to intervene appropriately.

Clashes between Extraverts and Introverts

Extraverts will usually want to externalise the disagreement so that it can then become a point of discussion. Remember, extraverts think with their mouths and so they will want to talk through the issue. As they talk, so they may shift their position - even to such an extent that sometimes they won't remember what they said earlier! This can lead to further conflict. If they are also Judgers, then Extraverts may find themselves arguing for points of view that they don't necessarily hold, but Judgers often find it difficult to adjust their position (even when they know that they are wrong). When Introverts are arguing with Extravert Judgers they need to remember that EJs already know the answer - its just that sometimes they can't remember the question!

Introverts, on the other hand, deal with conflict by internalising it. They work out their next move in their heads and take care not to say anything that they will regret later. Above all, they stay cool and aloof.

So, in a conflict between the two, Extraverts will tend to fill in the spaces and the Introverts will become even quieter. The differences in personality type may well aggravate the tension between them, irrespective of how they deal with the original point of contention.

Conflict between Sensers and Intuitives

The principal difference between these two types revolves around how they take in information. Sensers want precision and Intuitives want impressions. So what is likely to happen when there is a difference between them is that 'facts' become the focus for dispute. Sensers will want to concentrate on specifics and Intuitives will become impatient with detail and may become even more generalised. Similarly Sensers will become frustrated by the Intuitive's lack of precision and their seeming inability to deal with the present situation.

Conflict between Judgers and Perceivers

Judgers like structure, so any unplanned or unannounced changes can take them by surprise and lead them to give an abrasive response, which can be interpreted as anger but may not necessarily be so. Closure is important for Judgers and in seeking closure they can give the impression of sounding right, of being clear and certain - especially if they are also extravert. Judgers tend to want other people to be like themselves.

Perceivers, on the other hand, dislike closure and want to keep their options open. The more they are pressurised the less likely they are to reach a firm conclusion; or they may reach one and then change their mind, to the added annoyance of Judgers.

Disagreements within the same type

Of course conflict does not only occur between people of differing type, it can also happen between people who share similar personality types.

When two Extraverts disagree there can be fireworks! The disagreement can escalate as both parties make even more extravagant claims. On the other hand, the disagreement can be quickly sorted out and both parties quickly and easily turn their attention to other things.

Conflict between Introverts can simmer on for a long time, with neither party finding it easy to bring things out into the open. There will be a tendency for them both to brood over things and there may well be need for someone else in the team to intervene and help them to bring differences to the surface and discuss them.

Disagreements between Sensers can get locked into a repetition of facts and the digging up of more and more facts. Sensers may lack the imaginative skills to find a way out of their dilemma and although they may want to get things settled they may find it impossible to find a way forward. They will need the help of an Intuitive to come up with a novel way of turning lose-lose into win-win.

Intuitives falling out with each other respond by not dealing with it. They are not so adept at sorting out things in the present, preferring to imagine future possibilities. As neither of them will be totally sure of their facts, having intuited their reading of the situation, they may be reluctant to bring the dispute out into the open as they may have problems in remembering the exact details relating to the cause of the dispute. They may need the help of an extravert Senser in order to sort out just what are the facts behind their disagreement.

Feelers seldom have disputes! They both want harmony, they both want to be liked and valued and they both have difficulties in being tough and objective. So when there are (inevitable) disagreements they are likely to internalise them - or one person internalises their hurt/disagreement and the other lets them. When two Feelers do have an open conflict it is likely to be extremely deep and painful, of a magnitude probably quite out of all proportion to the actual problem. This is because neither of them really knows how to handle their anger and so it is stored up until it boils over. When it breaks out there may be months and months of all sorts of other hurts also mixed up with this one and coming out in one single deluge. Probably best to duck - there will be little chance of a rational response!

When Thinkers disagree with each other there will be a lot of analysing and competing for the logical superiority. If they are Extraverts as well there may be quite a lot of anger; if they are Introverts there may be a distinct coolness in the atmosphere. They may find it quite difficult to become reconciled as they lack the feeling skills and the empathy to transcend the gulf between them. Sarcasm may become a tactic.

When Judgers are in conflict there can be a real battle for power, with both parties being convinced that they are in the right. There can also be a danger that an over-quick resolution to the problem is found, with both sides looking for early closure, however, innate stubbornness may mean that the dispute drags on with neither party being willing to give way. In a hierarchical organisation things may be settled by appealing to status, or to some external authority.

Disputes between Perceivers are often not addressed, both sides preferring to move onto something else rather than face up to something which might require a resolution and closure. Perceivers basically want to enjoy life and want to bring a sense of fun and spontaneity into their work situation, therefore they will tend to avoid situations which require them to have to face up to the responsibilities brought on by their taking on too many jobs and not finishing any, or most, of them in the time agreed. They may need help to disentangle themselves from the consequences of poor time management, saying 'yes' to too many people and not making decisions at the appropriate times.

Each personality type brings certain strengths into the work situation, but each one also brings certain weaknesses.

This is why it can be helpful to move the focus of conflict away from the 'person' and see it in terms of their personality type.

Because the Myers Briggs Type Indicator is built upon people's preferences, it goes without saying that if I prefer one end of the spectrum then I might be irritated by someone who shows (to my mind) the excesses of the other end.

This section gives you some handy hints about how to deal with those irritating features which we discover in other people. It may also help them to come to terms with some of the irritating features that they find in you!

How to keep Extraverts from externalising everything
- ❋   encourage them to ask themselves a few more questions
- ❋   in meetings, suggest that they listen rather more and speak rather less
- ❋   in discussions or meetings, build in time for quiet reflection (a couple of minutes quiet to think about what is being discussed, or to write down your own thoughts)

How to keep Introverts from isolating themselves

* encourage them to ask other people a few more questions, to check out their understanding with other people's
* in meetings, suggest that they speak rather more (if you can, draw them out at meetings, ask them questions)
* in discussions or meetings, build in time for interaction (buzz groups)

How to keep Sensers from getting stuck on specifics

* think of a fundamental reason why this change should be made
* emphasise the sensory origin of the idea (eg it came from something that you have *seen* elsewhere)
* find a short and memorable way in which to communicate your ideas
* give them an action plan, spelling out the sequence of the changes planned
* see if there is something similar in existence somewhere else - Sensers feel less threatened if someone else has tried it first
* check out your ideas with another Sensing friend first, before you communicate them to the Senser

How to keep Intuitives from never leaving never-never land

* encourage them to talk about their vision before you give them your details
* set your ideas within the context of when they were new and exciting
* give them the overall framework before you start on the details
* don't judge your progress by tangible results but by the development of your concepts and ideas
* to get Intuitives grounded, throw them a line and gently lead them, don't try to shoot them down

How to keep Thinkers from trampling all over other people's feelings

 ❋ don't respond to them when your feelings are strong - you might become emotional or illogical
 ❋ make it clear just what it was that caused the original hurt or anger
 ❋ listen to their side and let them know that you understand their position
 ❋ explain your (or other people's) feelings in objective terms, and show the logic of them
 ❋ suggest or explore alternative ways of expressing themselves

How to keep Feelers from failing to deal with the 'tough stuff'

 ❋ don't give feedback when you are feeling very critical
 ❋ prepare the conversation by listing first all the things that they do well
 ❋ use the word *'and'* rather than the word *'but'*
 ❋ be co-operative and helpful
 ❋ help them to see the various impersonal factors that are at work in any situation, so that they do not interpret everything as being some sort of judgement on themselves

How to keep Judgers from jumping to conclusions

 ❋ give them new information in advance so that they can spend time thinking about it and preparing themselves
 ❋ acknowledge the value of their judgements beneath their annoying style
 ❋ make it quite clear to them when you are speculating or thinking aloud, and when you consider that they are doing the same
 ❋ ask them questions about their decision processes, encourage them to spell out how they have reached a particular conclusion
 ❋ let them organise data collection and reviews - this plays to their strengths

How to keep Perceivers from persistently procrastinating

❀ give them plans in advance and encourage them to spend time thinking about them

❀ acknowledge the value of all the additional information that they bring up, beneath their annoying style

❀ make it clear when you have made a decision, have set a deadline or are about to act, and when you want them to do the same

❀ ask them questions which make them think about the order and direction of their thoughts and the processes behind their decision making (or non decision making)

❀ arrange frequent feedback sessions - they have a tendency to move off into different areas and you (and they) need to be kept informed about their current concerns

The Personality of Organisations

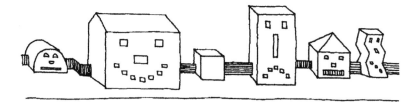

Just as individual people have their own personalities, so too organisations can be said to have their own culture or personality. Much less work has been done in this area than in the area of profiling the personality of individuals, and so the material is rather more impressionistic, but nonetheless the work done so far has thrown up some interesting insights. In terms of how teams operate it clearly makes a difference whether the team is a surgical unit working in a cardiology department of a hospital or whether it is planning the brochure for a tour operator - both are important but their needs may differ. It may therefore be helpful to think for a moment or two about your own organisation and how this affects the ways in which you work.

Extraverted organisations
- have open boundaries
- allow access to decision making
- collaborate on decisions
- act quickly
- experiment with several possible lines of action
- trust oral communication
- encourage internal co-operation
- turn to outsiders for guidance
- seek assistance when in trouble
- invite outsiders to celebrations

Introverted organisations
- have closed boundaries
- prevent access to decision making
- reach consensus after a decision is made
- explore options in detail, then take one line of action
- trust written communication
- experience internal mistrust
- insist that guidance should come from within
- batten down the hatches when in trouble
- keep celebrations 'within the family'

Sensing organisations
- are at their best with detail
- can handle masses of data
- prefer well established routines
- prefer change to come gradually
- make improvements (rather than major surgery)
- see Intuitive organisations as being lost in the clouds and basically untrustworthy
- see the future as an extension of the present
- emphasise targets and plans
- trust experience and authority

Intuitive organisations
- are best with the big picture
- can spot emerging trends
- are a little careless about routines
- prefer transformational (dramatic and far-reaching) change
- change paradigms/belief systems
- see Sensing organisations as being stuck in the mud
- believe that the future can be created
- emphasise purposes and vision
- trust insight and creativity
- understand that people may work in spurts of enthusiasm and that there may be fallow periods in between

Feeling organisations
- make decisions based on values
- think in terms of particular human situations
- value what we care about
- emphasise the people
- believe that support leads to effectiveness
- encourage members to do their best
- are a social community

Thinking organisations
- make decisions based on principles
- think in terms of rules and exceptions
- value what is logical
- emphasise the objective
- believe that criticism leads to efficiency
- encourage members to live up to the organisation's expectations
- are a social machine

Judging organisations
- drive towards decisions and objectives
- may be weak in information gathering
- set clear, specific standards
- define lots of things in detail
- are often moralistic

Perceiving organisations
- keep options open and seek more information
- may be weak in decision taking
- set general standards
- leave many things vague and undecided
- are loose and fairly tolerant

14   Type, Temperament and Teams

Using the Myers Briggs Personality Indicator, with its four distinct axes

Extravert - Introvert	Sensing - Intuition
Thinking - Feeling	Judging - Perceiving

means that we can finish up with sixteen different types of personality profile and anyone completing a full MBTI questionnaire will be given and will have discussed with them, their own distinct profile. The sixteen are:

ISTJ	*ISFJ*	*INFJ*	*INTJ*
ISTP	*ISFP*	*INFP*	*INTP*
ESTP	*ESFP*	*ENFP*	*ENTP*
ESTJ	*ESFJ*	*ENFJ*	*ENTJ*

Further work done on personality profiling (principally, in this case by Kiersey and Bates) has simplified things a little by suggesting that we can group certain types of personality together to produce different Temperaments. For a variety of reasons, beyond the scope of this publication, they argue for the following four temperaments:

NF	-	*Intuitive Feelers*
NT	-	*Intuitive Thinkers*
SP	-	*Sensing Perceivers*
SJ	-	*Sensing Judgers*

It is then possible to take these four categories and build up a *team member profile* for each one of them. Clearly, these are very broad profiles and it is unlikely that members of your team will find an exact match with them, but it is also likely that, in looking at them you will immediately recognise the value of using personality as a way of approaching teamwork.

The NF team member - the catalyst

NFs look at the world and see
> - possibilities, relationships and meanings

NFs focus on
> - the growth needs of the organisation

NF strengths include
> - drawing out the best in people
> - working with and through participative leadership
> - good verbal and listening skills
> - sensitivity to the climate of the organisation

Potential weaknesses of the NF
> - being too generous in giving time and self to others
> - basing decisions upon personal likes and dislikes
> - being too easily hurt and upset - personalising criticism
> - avoiding hard or hurtful decisions

NFs believe that
> - an organisation's strength is its people
> - an organisation must utilise people's gifts and skills

NFs need
> - approval from others
> - recognition as a person (who also happens to do
> a good job)

Questions that NFs ask
- how does this action/decision affect people?
- who needs to know?
- what is most important to the people?
- what impact do the decisions we take have on the organisation's principles or objectives?

NFs are irritated by
- impersonal treatment
- criticism
- lack of positive feedback

NFs irritate other people by
- taking emotional stands
- adopting moralistic positions
- getting over-extended
- creating dependency situations with others

NFs contribute to teams by
- adding the personal dimension
- being the advocate for a cause/policy/argument
- bringing out the contribution that others can make

The potential pitfalls of the NF are
- avoiding or denying problems
- having favourites
- always putting other people's priorities first
- being too anxious to please

The NT team member - the visionary

NTs look at the world and see
- possibilities, meaning and organisation

NTs focus on
- the mission and systems of the organisation

NTs strengths include
- looking ahead and seeing new possibilities
- building conceptual frameworks, especially relating to organisational change
- setting high standards
- seeing to the heart of complex issues

Potential weaknesses of the NT
- insensitivity to subordinates
- boredom with routine (they may not complete routine tasks if they are also Perceivers)
- losing people by their fascination for complexity
- impatience with those who seem to be incompetent

NTs believe that
- organisations should run according to their mission
- organisations should grow and develop

NTs need
- recognition for the quality of their ideas
- recognition for their professional competence

Questions that NTs ask
- what is involved?
- what is the strategy?
- who has the power?
- what is the system?
- where are we going?
- why?

NTs are irritated by
- stupid errors
- illogical actions
- unprofessionalism

NTs irritate other people by
- their scepticism
- their tendency to split hairs
- hurting people's feelings
- taking people's contributions for granted

NTs contribute to teams by
- problem solving skills
- providing a theoretical framework/input
- their contagious enthusiasm for ideas

The potential pitfalls of the NT are
- great strengths and great weaknesses
- lack of execution after the design stage
- impatience with human errors
- escalating standards

The SP team member - the trouble shooter

SPs look at the world and see
- facts
- realities

SPs focus on
- the expedient needs of the organisation

SPs strengths include
- handling crisis situations
- having a practical approach to concrete problems
- being adaptable and flexible
- being prepared to take risks

Potential weaknesses of the SP
- dislike of abstract, theoretical issues
- being unpredictable
- become bored without a crisis (beware - they may create one!)
- dislike writing
- dislike following set procedures

SPs believe that
- the most immediate is the most important
- the organisation must be run to meet current needs

SPs need
- to be appreciated for their ingenuity in getting things done
- a response

Questions asked by SPs
- what is the need right now?
- where is the crisis?
- when can we start?
- what are the stakes?
- what are our resources?

SPs are irritated by
- restrictions
- being told how to work
- systems *per se*
- having to report back

SPs irritate other people by
- their lack of follow-through
- their lack of preparation well in advance
- carelessness and haste
- overlooking established procedures and priorities

SPs contribute to teams by
- making things happen
- spotting practical problems
- negotiating agreements and plans of action

The potential pitfalls of the SP are
- being hard to predict
- their impatience with theory and abstraction
- their over-riding concern for the present
- ignoring the past and its implications for the future

The SJ team member - the traditionalist

SJs look at the world and see
- realities
- structure
- tradition

SJs focus on
- the hierarchy of the organisation

SJ strengths include
- being realistic, practical and decisive
- paying attention to rules, regulations and detail
- being dependable and following things through
- being thorough, systematic and precise

Potential weaknesses of the SJ
- not always being responsive to the need for change
- deciding things too quickly
- being impatient with delays and complications
- allowing rules to determine vision and action

SJs believe that
- organisations run on solid facts and set procedure
- people (including themselves) must 'earn their keep'

SJs need
- to be appreciated for their careful accurate work
- appreciation for holding organisations together and maintaining traditions and standards

Questions asked by SJs
- what is the order?
- what is my duty?
- why change?
- how is this justified?
- does it work?

SJs are irritated by
- others not following standard procedures
- ignored deadlines
- irresponsibility, daydreaming, and undue flexibility
- uncertainty

SJs irritate other people by
- doom and gloom positions
- their apparent slavery to procedures
- commitment to hierarchies
- their sense of being 'right'

SJs contribute to teams by
- focusing upon what needs to be done
- making the organisation run smoothly
- focusing on follow-through
- being mindful of details
- remembering the 'history/culture' of the organisation

The potential pitfalls of the SJ are
- impatience when delays occur
- deciding things too quickly
- their belief that long and hard work is the only way to success
- their tendency towards organisational tyranny

15 Fifteen Reflections on Teams - in the light of the Myers Briggs Type Indicator

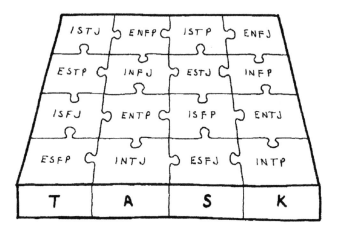

1   Teams with many members of similar types will probably come to understand each other quite quickly.

2   Teams with many similar types may make mistakes because the viewpoints that other types could offer are not represented.

3   Teams with a wide spread of types may take longer to reach agreement but may make decisions which are of better quality.

4   Teams with a narrow spread of types may compensate for this by ensuring that they involve other types who may not be team members; or they may choose quite deliberately not to think and act according to type and place themselves in the thought pattern of a different type.

5 Team members who are opposite to each other on all four preferences may have special difficulties in understanding or relating to each other.

6 A person who is the only representative of a particular type, the only Thinker, for example, may be seen as being 'different' by the others and may find themselves being marginalised.

7 Extraverts within the team may dominate discussions and decision taking unless they make a particular effort to involve Introverts.

8 Introverts in teams must make special efforts to be heard.

9 In teams which are dominated by Feelers there may be a strong emphasis on harmony and 'being a team'. This can, at times, have a detrimental effect upon the team's ability to achieve high standards or to deal with difficult issues/people.

10 In teams which are dominated by Thinkers, there may be a great commitment to 'fairness' and to the task in hand. Commitment to harmony and to 'teamness' may be sacrificed or ignored.

11 In teams where Sensers dominate there may be a great attention paid to detail and to systems but there may be a reluctance to make necessary changes and when things are going badly they may find it difficult to discover a way through their problems.

12 In teams where Intuitives dominate there may be a fascination with change and an eagerness to explore new ways, but they may find that they overlook important details.

13 Teams need Judgers to provide organisation, systematic thinking and decisiveness, but if Judgers dominate teams there may be a lack of flexibility and an overbearing sense of 'being right'.

14 Teams need Perceivers to provide them with openness, tolerance and flexibility, but if Perceivers dominate teams there may be a lack of decisiveness and a rather spineless structure.

15 Using Personality Types to understand teams and the ways in which they operate can free people from personalising conflict and provide them with a framework for obtaining facts, exploring possibilities, thinking through the consequences of different types of action and assessing the impact that their possible actions might have on other people.

16 My own personal reflection on teamwork processes

♦ What aspects of my work, and my contribution to the team do I wish to be noticed and appreciated by the other members?

a

b

c

d

♦ What are the things about this team which irritate me most? Can I understand them in terms of Personality Types, in terms of the strengths and weaknesses of myself and others?

a

b

c

d

- What aspects of my work and style are most likely to irritate the other members of the team? Is it possible to be specific about different aspects and different members?

  a   may be irritated by my ....

  b   may be irritated by my ....

  c   may be irritated by my ....

  d   may be irritated by my ....

- What type of people do I find it most difficult to work with, and how do I need to address the problems that arise?

  a

  b

  c

  d

- How would I assess the make-up of my team, and what three steps need to be taken to ensure that we work as efficiently and as effectively as possible?

  1

  2

  3